The 3 Secrets of Happiness: Forever Joy Can Be Yours

DR. ALEXANDER AVILA

Heart and Soul Publishing International

2017

ISBN-13: 978-1544662725

ISBN-10: 1544662726

Acknowledgements

Special thanks and love to:

Antonio, my father, The Great Philosopher: May your spirit rest in loving energy and peaceful joy.

My son, Andy, the Russian Missile: May you be a powerful force for good and light in the world.

My Creative Energizer, Robin Blakely: May the seed of love spread throughout our work together.

Praise for *The 3 Secrets of Happiness*

"In *The 3 Secrets of Happiness*, our mystic guru, Tanaka, guides us with a wise and sometimes 'tough-loving' hand through the labyrinth of misconceptions about happiness. With Tanaka's help, we emerge re-born, our egos having fallen away, with a profound understanding of the three secrets and how to nurture happiness in our daily lives. Great lessons indeed!"

Dr. Mary Jayne Rogers, author of *From Overwhelmed to Inspired: Your Personal Guide to Health and Well-Being*
www.doctormaryjayne.com.

TABLE OF CONTENTS

Chapter One

The 3 Secrets of Happiness

"Happiness," a wise master once said, "is only happiness if you don't know why it exists."

If you know why happiness exists, that means you have reasons for it. You have "Ifs" for happiness; you consider yourself happy *if* you meet certain conditions; *if* you experience particular circumstances in life. The dilemma is that there are many "Ifs" to happiness:

"If I have career or financial success, I will be happy."

"If I have good health and a loving family, I will be happy.

"If I achieve my goals, I will be happy."

"If I am a religious person, I will be happy."

Here is the problem: When you have reasons—Ifs—for your happiness, then you have equally compelling reasons—Ifs—for your unhappiness. If the relationship or finances goes sour, if the family fights, if your health fades, if you don't achieve your goals, if your religious faith declines—then your reasons for happiness can easily turn into reasons for unhappiness—into frustration, resentment, and sadness.

The truth is that real happiness does not depend on external conditions, specific reasons, or favorable circumstances. It does not depend on "Ifs." Happy people are happy, despite their circumstances in life, not because of them. Truly happy people live in conditions both good and bad; experiencing fortune both lucky and unlucky. Yet, through it all, they are still happy; happiness is within them.

Of course, it's a blessing to be healthy, have wonderful family and friends, make good money, enjoy a rewarding career, own attractive things, give to others, and so on. Those things can give you a satisfying sense of pleasure, success, and excitement; they can offer you a certain level of personal growth or temporary contentment. But, they cannot, by themselves, give you Happiness—the permanent, long-term, rock-solid, immovable, irreplaceable, and invincible sense of absolute joy that makes life worth living.

What is true happiness then? How can we attain it? Fortunately, we now have a solution to the happiness dilemma: The greatest psychologists and philosophers the world over have recently made great strides in researching and discovering the dynamics of human happiness. By carefully interviewing and studying the happiest people on earth, these leading social scientists have discovered what are now known as the three secrets of happiness.

Interestingly enough, these secrets do not involve the things that are usually considered important for attaining happiness. Fame, power, money, love, family, relationships, religion, health, or worldly success are not the determining factors of a happy life. In fact, the three secrets of happiness are not that complicated at all. They consist of three simple psychological traits, or attributes, that the happiest people in the world possess.

If you develop these three psychological traits, and practice them on a daily basis, you will be happy, no matter what else happens to you—despite any, and all, circumstances. Not only will you be happier, research shows, but you will also have a stronger immune system, be a better worker, earn more income, have a more satisfying marriage, be more sociable, and cope better with daily difficulties.

What, then, are these three marvelous secrets, or traits, of happiness? They are:

Gratitude
Joyful Optimism, and
Forgiveness.

You may already intuitively know the importance and power of these inner traits, but knowing these three secrets is not enough. You must embrace them; you must practice them; you must absorb them into your very being until they become you; until they act for you—automatically bringing you all of the wonderful blessings that life has to offer.

You will not become happy simply by learning about happiness as some abstract concept or idea. To be a happy person, you need to practice happiness as a daily habit. You need to observe and imitate people who are already genuinely happy. Do what happy people do, and you, too, will be happy.

The good news is that you now have an opportunity to learn from one of the greatest masters of happiness. You are about to meet a mentor who will guide you on your journey toward mastering the three secrets of happiness in your personal life. This sage, Master Tanaka, is prepared to teach you the three secrets of happiness. Are you ready to learn?

Chapter Two
The Amazing Story of Master Tanaka

There once was a wise and happy sage named Tanaka who lived in a remote wilderness mountain area. With long flowing hair, a hairless face, and features that were neither precisely male nor female, this Master Teacher was a mysterious figure indeed. For our purposes, we will refer to Tanaka as a man; although that is not certain, by any means. Tanaka could have been a man, or she could have been a woman. No one could really tell.

Tanaka's age was a mystery also. Some said Tanaka was in the middle years of life, others said Tanaka was very old, but looked much younger. People also had a hard time figuring out Tanaka's nationality. Some guessed Japanese, others said Native American, and still others said Latin of some sort. But, no one really knew the answers to these questions about Tanaka. The only thing that people knew for sure was that this happy-go-lucky sage exuded an extraordinary sense of gentleness, kindness, love, and happiness.

Tanaka lived in a modest way. He dressed simply, but elegantly, in clothes he made with his own hands. He tended to his garden, from which he received most of his daily sustenance. He also performed his martial arts exercises every morning without fail. Tanaka, in fact, was considered a gentle warrior—a martial arts master who could kill with a light touch of his hands, just as easily as he could heal with those same hands.

Some said Tanaka had been a very successful doctor who suffered a nervous breakdown after an especially difficult operation, and had given up the practice of medicine to become a hermit. Others said he came from a very wealthy family and had used his inheritance to travel the world, sampling the pleasures and sensualities of the earth, until he grew tired of it all and chose the simple, monastic life.

Regardless of the theory of how Tanaka became Tanaka, one thing was certain: He was a happy man. Always singing, laughing, and playing with animals or children, Tanaka was never seen sad, depressed, angry, irritated, or frustrated in any way. He also didn't seem to crave any type of worldly success or approval; any type of material accumulation. He seemed perfectly content with who he was and the way he lived.

One day, a famed psychiatrist, who specialized in treating the most difficult cases of schizophrenia, heard about Tanaka from one of his colleagues, and decided to investigate for himself. Through a mutual acquaintance, the psychiatrist, we'll call him Harry, arranged to meet Tanaka at his mountain residence to learn about Tanaka's "secrets of happiness."

Upon arriving at Tanaka's residence in his chauffeur-driven Mercedes, Harry was eager to get to work. Harry had brought his two secretaries, and special video recording equipment, to make sure everything they discussed was meticulously recorded.

Harry smiled as he thought about how his meeting with Tanaka would provide excellent material for a bonus chapter in his upcoming autobiography: "Lessons from the Master Shrink." The chapter would detail some of his theories on delusional behavior, and include his interview with Tanaka, the famous recluse who claimed to know the secrets of happiness. In fact, Harry decided, a great title for the chapter would be "The Hermit Who Claimed Happiness."

Whereupon Harry Meets Tanaka in a Most Unusual Way

Upon seeing Harry approach with his entourage and recording equipment, Tanaka came out of his modest home in a quite unexpected manner: He was completely and unashamedly naked. At this point, Tanaka did appear to be a man, as he was endowed in a certain well-proportioned manner that made an excellent case for maleness. Greeting Harry warmly, Tanaka calmly and sweetly said,

"Please send your friends and cameras over here so they can get a closer look at me."

Horrified at Tanaka's completely exposed and naked condition, Harry told his secretaries to wait in the car with the recording equipment as he mumbled, "Mr. esteemed Tanaka, is this a good time? I notice you are without clothes, and I have brought my assistants and some recording equipment. Please tell me what you would like to do?"

"Today, I like being in a natural state," replied Tanaka. "If your assistants aren't comfortable with that, please send them away with their recording equipment."

Reluctantly, Harry agreed with Tanaka's request to send his people away. Harry thought he might be dealing with a delusional schizophrenic—someone who was completely out of touch with reality. To be on the safe side, Harry told his assistants to wait nearby for his call, just in case he needed to leave earlier than planned.

"I know what you're thinking," Tanaka interrupted Harry's thoughts. "You think I must be a nut case or something. Actually, I like to eat nuts, but I'm not a nut case. If you look a little closer, you will see that I am not really naked. I simply hypnotized you into believing I was naked, so your assistants would leave and take their cameras with them. I don't like cameras; they are human ways of trying to capture reality, which can't be done because reality is only in the moment. Your assistants would also have gotten in the way of your learning because their reactions would have colored your own experience. Now, the obstacles have been removed, and you can learn with pure awareness."

"What the hell are you trying to pull?" asked an enraged and amazed Harry as he realized that he had, indeed, been tricked. Tanaka was, actually, fully clothed—he was wearing sandals and some type of homemade robe. Tanaka also had a mischievous grin on his face that made Harry feel even more irritated.

When Tanaka didn't answer (he just kept looking at Harry with that same silly grin), Harry tried again to get a response from Tanaka, this time using his most neutral professional tone. "Mr. Tanaka, you are indeed a very complicated man. I see that you're playing little tricks on me, but I really have no time for games. The clock is ticking. Do you know who *I* am?"

"Do you know who *I* am?" asked Tanaka as he burst into uncontrollable laughter, and began doing a strange little chicken dance—flapping his arms, making chicken sounds, and hopping and skipping with childish delight. It was an odd spectacle, thought Harry, but also strangely infectious, even somewhat endearing. But, right now, Harry wasn't in the mood for fun and games. This was serious; he was being challenged.

"I will tell you who I am!" thundered Harry in his deep patrician voice. "I am the esteemed Harry Johnson, premier psychiatrist, world-renowned for my work in the specialty area of paranoid schizophrenia. I have published and lectured extensively on the delusional schizophrenic, and I have thoroughly examined the abnormality of human nature. I have written several well-received textbooks in my field, and I have many honors."

"Stop it. Moron," said Tanaka.

"What did you say!?" replied an astonished Harry. No one had ever spoken to him like that before. Nobody dared.

"Idiot," said Tanaka, with a straight face.

"What the..." began Harry, desperately trying to contain himself.

"I don't mean it that way," said Tanaka, as his face broke out into one of the most beautiful, angelic smiles Harry had ever seen. Harry's anger evaporated just as quickly as it began, replaced by burning curiosity. This man, Tanaka, was definitely a most unusual sort of individual; he was certainly worth studying.

Tanaka continued in a soothing, conciliatory tone, "I see that you just reacted to the words I used ('moron' and 'idiot') in a very severe and angry way. Part of you (your false nature) identified with those words and reacted with defensiveness and hostility."

Harry realized what Tanaka was doing; using a psychological ploy to bait Harry into anger, then temporarily pacifying him, so Tanaka could keep the upper hand. It was a power and control game that Harry had played many times, and always won. Harry liked a mental challenge; he was going to enjoy the verbal chess game they were about to play.

"My dear Tanaka," said Harry. "You are a wiser man than I thought. You want to play with me to see how I will react. Very clever."

"My dear Harry," replied Tanaka with a shrewd wink. "You have it all wrong. You think I'm playing with you, when it's really you who are playing with yourself."

Harry quickly recoiled at Tanaka's use of words. He felt a sharp pain in his stomach. This Tanaka was tougher than he thought, Harry realized. Tanaka's words could soothe, but they could also burn.

"Harry," continued Tanaka, shedding more light on the subject, "the problem is that you are not taking your True Self seriously—the strong and secure part of your mind that is immune from the world's negative energy. Instead, you are reacting with your lower self—the weak, self-attacking part of you that vibrates and resonates to the bitterness, sarcasm, and insults of the world."

"Mr. Tanaka," said Harry in an irritated tone, "Let's cut the psychobabble crap and get to the point. You know the keys of happiness. Tell me: What are the secrets?"

Tanaka erupted with a deep belly laugh, and said, "You came all the way here just to ask me that? Who told you I knew the keys to happiness? I don't even know if I have the key to the restroom most of the time."

Harry could see that Tanaka was in love with his own jokes, so he decided to joke back. "You smell bad, Tanaka, maybe you don't have a bathroom around here."

Even before the words were fully spoken—as they halfway lingered in the air—Tanaka performed a lightning quick version of Okuri Ashi Harai (front foot sweep), taking out Harry's legs from under him, and sending Harry crashing to the ground. Yet, Harry didn't fall completely; Tanaka gently caught him by the shoulders and held him up lovingly, caressingly, just like a small baby. Harry even felt a little loved as he was cradled in Tanaka's arms.

"See how dependent you are on your fellow human beings?" asked Tanaka gently, with a caring lilt to his voice. "You need to find people who can sweep you off your feet, but who won't let you down." As Tanaka spoke, he tenderly carried Harry and carefully placed him in a chair under the shade of a tall pine tree.

Scared and impressed, Harry simply said the first words that came to mind: "Thank you."

Satisfied now that Harry had the right attitude to learn, Tanaka began the first lesson.

Chapter Three

The 3 Secrets of Happiness
Revealed

"You're right, Harry," began Tanaka. "There are certain special secrets, or keys, to happiness. I have found them. In fact, to make it simple for you, I will tell you about the three keys to happiness."

"Why only three?" asked Harry.

"I don't know why. Maybe there are three hundred. But, I don't think so. In all of my life, both on this earth, and in my spiritual intuition, I have found three absolute and irrevocable keys, or secrets, to achieving happiness in life.

"But, before I tell you what they are, I must first explain something very important to you. Realize this, Harry: To discover what happiness *is*, you must first learn what happiness *is not*."

"What do you mean?" asked Harry, somewhat puzzled.

Tanaka elaborated further, "Many people focus on the things they must have in life before they consider themselves to be happy: ambition, money, material acquisitions, love, sex, approval, fame, power, friends, relationships, religion, family, health, beauty, youth—the list goes on and on. They mistakenly focus on the external conditions for their happiness; on the things they believe they must have, or on the conditions they think they must fulfill, before they can be happy. Unfortunately, attaining these things doesn't actually bring them any closer to happiness, even though they keep hoping it will."

"But, isn't that the way to reach happiness, by achieving your goals and dreams?" asked Harry.

"It seems like that would be the way, but it isn't. You see, happiness does not consist of what you can get, but of what you can get rid of. Happiness begins with the words 'is not.' You must first find what happiness *is not* before you can discover what happiness *is*. You must first find, and delete, the things that don't make you happy—the outer circumstances and inner elements (thoughts and feelings) that make you unhappy—before you can attract the true essence, the beautiful nectar, of happiness."

"I kind of understand," said Harry.

"Kind of understand is not good enough," said Tanaka in a mild rebuke. "You must understand fully. I'll give you an example. Have you ever been in a bad relationship?"

Harry thought back to his two ex-wives. The term "bad" was an understatement. There was fighting, disrespect, and cheating in his previous marriages.

"Yes," said Harry.

"Harry, there is a universal truth about relationships," said Tanaka. "The more you cling to a bad relationship, the less likely you are to ever have a good relationship. People rarely change; you already know that from your past experiences. If the relationship is lousy from the beginning, it's likely to stay that way to the end—whether it lasts one year, ten years, or a lifetime. So, now you have a choice to make: Do you want a fantastic relationship or a lousy one? If you want the great relationship, you must first completely eliminate the bad relationship; you need to leave that incompatible person before you waste any more of your life on something that just doesn't work. Once you do that, you open up a space in the universe for the right person to come into your life—for the ideal relationship to be drawn to you, naturally and effortlessly. That's the way it is, Harry: Get rid of what makes you unhappy to get what makes you happy. Does that make sense to you?"

"Yes, it makes perfect sense," said Harry, finally realizing what Tanaka was trying to tell him.

"Now listen to me closely, Harry, because it's time for us to begin the true lessons of life. What I'm going to teach you is unlike anything you've ever learned in medical school, or in your practice, or from reading your endless books and journals. What I'm about to show you are the real secrets of happiness from a universal and eternal perspective. These are the time-honored traditions and secrets that have been passed down from grandparent to parent to child.

"Are you ready to learn?" asked Tanaka with bright and shining eyes that transferred, for a brief moment, all of the love and wisdom he had in his mind into the mind of his new student, Harry.

"Yes, teacher," replied Harry, mesmerized by the shining eyes.

Chapter Four
The First Secret: Gratitude

Tanaka picked up a pear and asked Harry, "What is this?"

"A pear," replied Harry.

"No. Idiot."

"You called me idiot, again."

"I didn't call *you* an idiot, Harry. I used the word 'idiot.' A word has nothing to do with the real you. It is only made up of letters—a man-made creation. There are no words in the ultimate end of life. The only reason you reacted with anger is that you associated yourself—your value and self-esteem—with that word. You believed that I was calling the essential 'You' an idiot; that I was devaluing you in some way; making you seem inferior. In reality, I wasn't devaluing you because, in the higher sense, there is no 'you' to devalue. The real YOU is something higher than a word, a label, or a concept."

"I know what you're getting at," said Harry, as he felt his confidence rising again. He was well read in the areas of esoteric philosophy and semantics; he could argue with the best of them. "You're talking about me being part of some sort of cosmic consciousness, where I'm part of the whole of humanity, so I become egoless. Is that what you're talking about?"

"Not quite, Harry," said Tanaka, as he sensed that Harry wanted to engage him in a petty verbal battle. When will he learn? thought Tanaka. Now was the time. "Words will always fail you, my friend," continued Tanaka. "Words only carry part of the truth. Yes, there is such a thing as a higher or universal sense of self that goes beyond your very limited ego, what you call your *self*. But, you can't define it with mere words.

"You see, the verbal concepts you have in your mind (the ones you've learned from books) have very little to do with this ultimate self—this Superior Mind. But, if you could describe it with mere words, Harry, let's just say that this would be an incredibly beautiful exalted nature, a higher state of thinking and feeling, that would move you from an "I" to a "We" mentality—integrating, deep within you, the collective love and passion of God and every being on earth—making you whole, unified, and free; keeping you safe from insults, attacks, and criticisms of any kind."

As Tanaka spoke, he could see that Harry was drifting into deep thought; relaxing his mind; opening it up to new possibilities. This was good, thought Tanaka.

"I could go on for hours on this topic," continued Tanaka, "but, that is a lecture for another day. Let's proceed now with the truth of today's lesson. You asked me about the secrets of happiness, and I said there are three. I will start with the first secret: Gratitude.

"Gratitude is the feeling of overabundance in the present moment. It is expressing a feeling of thankfulness for all that God has provided, not just to you, but to everyone and everything around you.

"When I asked you what was in my hand, you said, 'pear,' and you were only half-right. It is actually a gift from the universe; a miracle from God; a blessing to us in this very moment. A pear—sustenance, food, life—and it's all ours right now."

"I know feeling grateful is important for happiness," said Harry. "But, it's often so hard to do. I worry endlessly about many things— my practice, my lover, my children, my friends. I feel overwhelmed much of the time. Many times I can't seem to enjoy my life, although I'm very financially successful, and many would say I'm also quite successful in my personal life as well."

Harry couldn't quite believe how open he was being with Tanaka. He was rarely that open with anyone. Even his lover, Jane, often struggled to get Harry to communicate the things he held deep inside. But, Tanaka's gentle and accepting ways made Harry feel like he could say anything; Harry knew he could speak from the heart in Tanaka's presence.

"Harry, I know exactly what you're feeling, what you're thinking," said Tanaka, as he paused for a moment, softly stroking his long flowing hair. "That's precisely why Gratitude is so important. It brings us back to the Present Moment. You see, many of us don't live in the Now. We live in constant expectation and worry about the future; we live in the disappointments and regrets of the past. In the meantime, we forget the sweet pleasure, the wonderful sensations, of the Present Moment."

"Yes, I understand what you're saying," said Harry as he took in a deep breath of fresh air and enjoyed the warm sun on his skin. "I've read the popular books on living in the now. It's a great idea, and it sounds wonderful on paper, but living in the now seems like such a difficult thing to do in the real world of problems, deadlines, and time pressures."

"It's not difficult at all, Harry; people just make it seem that way. Try this: Look around here, in my garden right now. Find something you like, something you find appealing, no matter how small or seemingly insignificant it may be. Go ahead, let your eyes wander, and tell me what you have found."

Harry looked around and found an interestingly shaped rock with a pretty color that he liked.

"This rock here, I like the way it looks," said Harry.

"Good," said a pleased Tanaka. "Now, thank the rock for being in your life. Go ahead. Thank it."

Harry felt silly doing this. "Come on, I can't talk to a rock. If I do, I'll be as crazy as you are, and I'll lose my license to practice medicine. I'm only joking, Tanaka. Don't take me seriously."

"Why should I take you seriously?" asked Tanaka with twinkle in his eye. "You already take yourself too seriously as it is. Now, Harry, give yourself permission to act a little crazy once in a while. Think about some of the great people who have been called crazy in our world:

Einstein, Edison, Gandhi, Mother Theresa, Madame Curie, Florence Nightingale, Martin Luther King. They all thought differently, and some people at the time thought they were crazy or weird; but look at how much they contributed to the world. So Harry, be a little crazy now, and thank that rock."

"OK, thank you, rock," said Harry, without much conviction at all. He wasn't fooling anyone, and he knew it.

"No, you're not really being grateful," scolded Tanaka. "You're not putting any real effort into this. You didn't even look the rock in the eye."

"What, are you kidding me? Rocks don't have eyes."

"How do you know? In its own way, maybe it does. May it can see right through you."

"Yeah, and now you're going to tell me that rocks are real beings. Is that what you think?"

"Of course, they're real," said Tanaka emphatically. "That rock you're holding in your hand right now is real. It was put here by God's touch—God's hand—on this earth for this very moment when you would pick it up and act like a jackass when I asked you to be grateful for it. How much realer can that get?"

"You're serious, aren't you?" asked Harry. In many ways, Harry still considered himself a skeptic. But, he also recognized there was much about the universe he didn't yet understand. Perhaps, Tanaka knew hidden truths that could change Harry's life. Maybe, it was about time Harry started listening.

Tanaka sensed Harry's doubts, but he also saw Harry's relentless inner drive for true knowledge; for personal freedom. Tanaka continued the lesson, "Yes, Harry, I'm very serious when it comes to

Gratitude. It's very important to us. We were brought into this life to enjoy all of God's creations, and to experience the great joy of Gratitude. Now, try again, Harry: Thank that rock for being here. Feel the gratitude. This time, really feel it."

This time, Harry looked at the rock differently. He saw it as an off-spring of the Life Force—the energy of God. He picked up the rock gingerly, lovingly, and spoke to it with real emotion, "Thank you, rock, for being in my life. You look very pretty to me; you give me pleasure. And, you know what? Right now, I have a strong desire to kiss you, rock."

Harry actually gave the rock a kiss, and turned to Tanaka. "You know, Tanaka, I realize this may look foolish, but I kind of like this rock. I'm really feeling grateful for its presence in my life."

"Harry, you are kind of crazy," said Tanaka, as he slowly shook his head. "I didn't tell you to kiss a rock. It's dirty; that's really disgusting."

"But, you told me..."

Tanaka interrupted him with booming laughter, "Again you're taking things too seriously, my friend. Yes, it's wonderful that you felt grateful for the rock, and that you wanted to kiss the rock. Do you want to make love to it, too?"

"Don't be ridiculous," said Harry, as his face start flushing. "I don't..."

"Let's be clear about this," explained Tanaka intently, "making love is not simply a physical act between two human beings. You can also make love to the world, not with your sex organs, but with your head, with your heart, with your soul. Look at that gorgeous bird over there, perched high up on that tree, with those beautiful feathers—how majestic and serene. Now, make love to that bird with your heart right now. See yourself joining with that bird as it flies into the sky, and you fly with it."

"Yes, I can see that; I can imagine that," replied Harry. He really could imagine it, and it felt good.

"And, look further out; look at the expanse of that beautiful blue sky. Use your imagination now and make love with that endless sky. Wrap your lips and your arms around that great big blue sky, and say 'I love you, Big Blue Sky.'"

"I love you, Big Blue Sky," said Harry, really feeling love for the sky, for the trees, for the birds, and even for the dirty rock he had just kissed. He still felt a bit strange, but he was becoming more comfortable with being grateful for everything around him.

"Now Harry, think about this: If you just felt love toward these inanimate objects and animals, imagine how much more love and gratitude you can express for your fellow human beings, for all the loved ones in your life, and for everyone else on this grand earth of ours.

"And, imagine how grateful you can feel for all the wonderful things you have right now: clothes, food, shelter, money, possessions, career, and relationships—your health, your breath, even your very life. How much more gratitude can you feel?"

Harry was suddenly overcome by a wave of gratitude and love as he pictured all of the things he was truly grateful for: an amazing woman in his life, his two beautiful children, his loyal friends, his patients, his successful psychiatry practice, his relatively good health, his outstanding financial status, his home, his cars, his yearly Caribbean vacations, his articles and books, all the people he's helped and touched over the years.

Tears of gratitude filled Harry's eyes. "Yes, I am grateful, teacher. I see what Gratitude truly is. It is living in the now, in the present moment; having a sincere appreciation and deep caring for all living things; for all nonliving entities; for all the wonder, love, and passion that human beings can experience on this earth, for having the greatest gift of all: Life."

"Yes, my son; you have truly learned the first Gift of Life: GRATITUDE.

"Practice this key constantly. It is yours to enjoy. With gratitude, your heart fills to the brim every day. You live in the present moment; you are thankful for everything you experience, even for the irritating and bothersome aspects of life.

"It's important to be grateful for the good things in life, Harry, but it's equally important to be grateful for the so-called bad things. That's really where you strengthen and perfect your Gratitude; when you are grateful for the things you normally find annoying and unpleasant.

"Start today, Harry. Be grateful for that traffic jam because it gives you extra time to listen to music, meditate, think, or pray. Be grateful for that rude and inconsiderate person because he or she gives you the opportunity to practice the higher principles of patience and tolerance. Every rude or obnoxious remark from that person is another reminder of how *not* to be. The rude person shows you how to be kind; the pushy person teaches you how to be gentle.

"Gratitude is really simple to practice. All you have to do is be grateful for everything that happens to you—whether you call it important or unimportant, good or bad, Gratitude covers all.

"To help you become even more grateful, try the following:

"Each morning as soon as you wake up, repeat the following words; say them out loud: 'I am grateful for my breath, for my life. I am grateful for this day. I am grateful for all that I have experienced, for all I will experience. I am grateful for those I love because true love keeps growing and growing. I am grateful for those I hate because they teach me compassion and forgiveness. I am grateful for all of my successes today, for they are my inheritance from God. I am grateful for all of my failures today because they are the Universe's way of keeping me humble so that when I do experience ultimate success and triumph, I will appreciate it even more.'

"Make up your own phrases, Harry. But, remember to be grateful for everything that happens to you, for everything you experience, whether you call it good or bad. It doesn't matter what you call it. Gratitude doesn't discriminate between things; it doesn't distinguish between events. It is a pure flowing feeling of joy, peace, love, serenity, and excitement—all wrapped up in one delicious package: Gratitude. With Gratitude in your heart, you will never lose."

Chapter Five
The Second Secret: Joyful Optimism

"I'm so grateful I came here to see you today, Teacher."

"That's the spirit, Harry. Gratitude is wonderful, but it's not enough. We humans need something else to truly be happy."

"What is that, teacher?" asked Harry, with increasing curiosity and excitement. He sincerely wanted to know all of the secrets of happiness—every single one.

"Joyful Optimism is the answer," said Tanaka. "Some call it faith, hope, expectations of a better day. Whatever you call it, Joyful Optimism is the perfect cure for anxiety; the perfect remedy for those who are afraid of the future."

Now, Harry was confused. He wanted some clarification "But, teacher, when we discussed Gratitude, I thought you emphasized the importance of focusing on the now, instead of the future."

"Not exactly, Harry," explained Tanaka patiently. "I said Gratitude deals with the present. However, the future is always ever-present in the minds of men and women. We must deal with it, somehow. But, the trouble is that most people deal with the future wrongly; they either become too excited about it, or they fear it—worrying endlessly about what will happen to them. Of course, neither is the correct response. Being overly excited about the future, for example, only sets you up for failure, as you fall under the influence of the universal law of human nature known as the Pendulum Principle."

"What is that, teacher?"

"I'll give you an example," offered Tanaka. "In my pocket, I have a gold nugget worth $10,000. I would like to give it to you for being my guest today, and for listening to the ramblings of an old fogey. How do you feel about that?"

"Are you sure you want to give me that, teacher?" replied Harry humbly. "The nugget is worth a lot of money."

"Yes, I'm sure," insisted Tanaka. "Here, please take it; you would make me very happy if you did." Tanaka took out a large nugget of shiny gold from his pocket and gave it to Harry.

"Thank you, I'm very grateful," said Harry, beaming with gratitude after receiving such a valuable gift from his generous teacher.

"What will you do with the nugget? I insist that you sell it and buy anything you want with it."

"Well," replied Harry, excitedly, "I could take my partner, Jane, on another one of those fantastic cruises we love—a Caribbean delight. Or, I could buy my son some of the guitar equipment he's been craving, or..."

"Harry."

"Yes?"

"It's not real."

"What?"

"The nugget I just gave you is fool's gold. It's fake. It's not real. It has no value."

"You son of a..." said Harry, with rumbling anger coming from the pit of his stomach.

"Now, be careful," warned Tanaka, as he pointed his trained hands toward Harry. "Would you like another demonstration of my fast reflexes and sharp movements?"

"No, thanks," replied Harry quickly, recalling his last martial arts encounter with Tanaka, a particularly unpleasant experience he wasn't eager to repeat. Warily, he spoke, "No disrespect intended, teacher, but you fooled me with the gold nugget. You had me thinking one way, that I would get the gold, and then you switched it on me, and then…" a light shone in Harry's eyes—he finally got it. "You were doing this to prove a point, weren't you, teacher? It's the Pendulum Principle."

"Correct, Harry; now you're learning. In fact, you're learning two important points. First, you're discovering how to stop your Anger in the moment it occurs; you're executing a Stop Thought—as the fiery and negative thought attacks you, you stop it right there in its tracks. This gives you more confidence and power to stop negativity the next time it rears its ugly head. Second, you've tapped into what the Pendulum Principle is all about. The Pendulum Principle is all about highs and lows, and it works like this:

"Something exciting happens to you. You get a raise, make some unexpected money, or meet an attractive person. Now, you momentarily feel good about yourself. You're excited, animated; you even call this happiness. Guess what? You're now at the top swing of the pendulum; you can do no wrong; you're on top of the world and a million other clichés.

"But, then the pendulum swings down. The raise comes with new responsibilities at work you don't want; the unexpected money tempts you into spending beyond your means; the attractive person turns out to be a dud. Nothing works out the way you planned; now you feel disappointed and frustrated.

"And, Harry, here's the worst part: Even if the raise gave you enough money, and the date was wonderful, you're still going to experience the pendulum principle at some point—when the high of the thrill wears off—when you come back down to your regular state of being. No matter how nice the prize or circumstance was, you will still inevitably suffer from a certain sense of emptiness that takes over once the initial excitement and thrill vanish."

"I can see that," realized Harry. "Excitement can't sustain itself. I saw how quickly I moved from excitement to anger when I realized the gold nugget wasn't real. Even if the prize turns out good, excitement must always move in the other direction at some point, turning into boredom, disappointment, frustration, and yearning."

"Exactly, Harry. And, guess what? Here's the kicker: What goes up must come down in equal proportion to how high it was. In other words, if you experience an excitement level of +99 from the prospect of receiving the gold nugget, then you're going to swing down to a level of -99 on the negativity scale—suffering from emotions like anger and frustration—when you realize the gold nugget is a fake. It happens every time: Whatever high you get from an external source will eventually result in an equally low level of discomfort and dissatisfaction once the psychological scale shifts in the opposite direction."

"That explains a lot of my life up to now," said Harry. "Even if I get a great result or have a wonderful experience, I often feel empty and let down afterwards, maybe not at the moment I get that pleasure or acquisition, but definitely later on that night, or that week, or that month. It happens to me all the time."

"Of course, Harry. That is the Pendulum Principle," explained Tanaka. "It's the inevitable result of False Excitement."

"False excitement?" asked Harry.

"False excitement," Tanaka elaborated further, "is not true lasting pleasure like self-mastery, spiritual love, compassion, and peace. False excitement is a temporary elation brought about by an external result or situation that you momentarily call 'good.' It's not necessarily good at a deep level; it just appears good because it's new, it's exciting, it's fresh. Then, once the newness, novelty, and excitement wear off, what you have left is the other side of the coin—craving, disappointment, and despair."

"How can we get around the Pendulum Principle, teacher?"

"Simple," replied Tanaka, smiling. He liked it when students asked intelligent questions. "First, we need to recognize exactly how the Pendulum Principle works, the way it jerks us from excitement to emptiness and back again. We need to learn how to refuse the false excitement it offers us when it tries to seduce us with pleasant visions of the future; with false promises, hopes, and expectations.

"Instead of basing our lives on the flimsy promises of an exciting, yet hazy future, we need to ground ourselves on the rock-solid steadiness of the present Now, on feeling grateful for the present moment. Being grateful in the now keeps us pleasantly occupied with the blessings of the present, and prevents us from getting too excited about fantasy images and unrealized possibilities that exist in some nebulous future."

Tanaka was warming up now. He continued to enlighten Harry. "A second way to defeat the Pendulum Principle is through Joyful Optimism—the God-given sense of well-being and contentment that tells us that everything is going to be all right, no matter what. With Joyful Optimism in our lives, we are certain the future will turn out perfectly fine for us, just the way the Universe intended it— without us having to add our own extraneous hopes, expectations, worries, fears, and excitement to the mix. We can relax because the future will come to us; we don't have to go to the future."

Harry couldn't help but smile. "Teacher, I'm excited about what you're teaching me. I know it's the right type of excitement because I'm learning the smart way to handle life." Tanaka nodded in agreement. "I see how the Pendulum Principle is our enemy, and Gratitude and Joyful Optimism are the friends who can help us defeat the Pendulum Principle. But, earlier, you also talked about another scourge of humanity: Fear of the future. Can you elaborate on that, teacher? How does fear trap humans?"

Shaking his head sadly, Tanaka replied:

"Fear of the future is humanity's never-ending curse; it dominates the minds of all human beings on earth. It doesn't matter what religion people are, what color skin they have, what country they're from—human beings all have one thing in common: They're obsessed, preoccupied, and frightened about the future—always anxious, always worried—as they ask the one question that is constantly burning on their minds: 'What will happen to me?'

"Harry, you want to know something? That one simple question, 'What will happen to me?' contains the seed for all the worry, all the anxiety, all the fear, that lie dormant in human minds. By asking that question, humans unconsciously sense that they are about to lose something valuable in their lives—something that will diminish their sense of self-esteem, their sense of worth. What are humans afraid of losing? Everything imaginable: their health, their looks, their youth, their money, their possessions, their abilities, their way of life, their intelligence, their loved ones, their reputation, even their very lives. They're. Afraid. Of. Losing."

"Is there anything we can do about that?" asked Harry with true concern in his voice. "Is fear our destined inheritance as human beings?"

"Good question, Harry. No, fear is not our final destination, as long as we apply the solution known as Joyful Optimism—two simple words that pack great power."

"Can you tell me more about Joyful Optimism, teacher?" asked Harry.

"It's very simple, really," said Tanaka. "Joyful optimism is the God-given belief, the absolute knowledge, that life will turn out just fine—that you will receive the bountifulness that the Universe has to offer. Think back to what Jesus said in the New Testament: 'Therefore I tell you, do not worry about your life, what you will eat or drink; or about your body, what you will wear… Can any one of you by worrying add a single hour to your life? And why do you worry about clothes? See how the flowers of the field grow. They do not labor or spin. Yet I tell you that not even Solomon in all his splendor was dressed like one of these.'

"The message of Jesus was simple, Harry," continued Tanaka. "Thinking about your life, worrying about it, won't make you any taller, prettier, richer, or happier. The only thing you have to do right now is to stop worrying about your life, and realize that God will provide everything. Even the clothes you wear on your back will be provided by God. Everything will work out perfectly fine as long as you believe that it will."

Tanaka was just getting started. He could barely contain his own excitement and enthusiasm as he continued sharing the power of

Optimism with Harry. "Joyful Optimism is incredible, Harry! It's the absolute cure for whatever ails you. Do you have job troubles, love troubles, or health troubles? No problem. Joyful Optimism will get you back on the right track—helping you feel better about yourself, encouraging you to take more of the right actions; giving you the willpower and confidence to attract all of the truly good things in your life."

"But, I already have joyful optimism," said Harry with an unconvincing look on his face. "I really do."

Looking deep within Harry's soul, Tanaka knew the truth that Harry wasn't admitting to himself.

"No, Harry, you know that's not true: Joyful optimism is not your daily companion. If it was, you wouldn't be here now, looking for the secrets of happiness. You would have already recognized those answers within yourself. You would not need me. You would live your life in joyous optimism every minute of every day—not knowing when or how the blessings will come, but knowing with unconditional certainty, that they *will* come. Knowing it just as you know I am standing here right before you, at this very moment."

"You're right, teacher," said an abashed Harry. "I don't have Joyful Optimism. I've been fooling myself into thinking I did have it. But, how can I get it?"

"You don't have to get it," replied Tanaka. "You already have it."

"Can you explain, teacher?"

"Listen, Harry: Joyful Optimism is inside the heart and soul of every living being. It is part of the DNA that God put inside each and every one of us. It's like saying we humans lack a heart, a brain, or a lung.

The truth is that we don't lack these essential organs; God gave them to us because we need them to keep us alive.

"In the same way, our DNA for Joyful Optimism is what keeps us emotionally alive and healthy in this chaotic and dangerous world of ours. It keeps us absolutely free from the painful and destructive influence of negative people, and it liberates us from our own negative thoughts and feelings."

"Why, then, do so few people manifest this Joyful Optimism in their lives?" asked Harry.

"Because humans are asleep, dreaming they're awake," replied Tanaka with a hint of sadness. "They think they're living true and authentic lives when all they're really doing is going through the motions. They sleep, eat, defecate, procreate, work a little, and then start the whole sordid mess all over again the next day. They are robots dreaming they are humans."

"How can they wake up?" asked Harry with intense interest. He wanted to know the answer; he *needed* to know.

"By listening to the beat of their hearts—the drums of their Joy!" proclaimed Tanaka with a passionate look in his eyes. "By finding and enjoying the true authentic pleasures of life—the small things that bring them natural joy and happiness: communing with nature, spending quality time with family and good friends, playing with animals and children, making love while being in love; meditating, praying, and connecting with God; creating, laughing, and loving. Whatever gives them natural and authentic pleasure is a key to that joy; to that perpetual optimism and openness they had when they were children.

"Yes, Harry, children are the truest, purest expression of Joyful Optimism. Children, God bless them, haven't yet been spoiled by the conformity, falsehood, hatred, and fear of much of society. They still hope; they still dream; they still believe. That is the spirit of childhood: fun, authentic, true, natural, and full of joyful optimism."

"Teacher, I've heard all of this before," said Harry with a sudden tone of cynicism. "Yes, I know: Children are supposed to be happy, joyous, playful, blah, blah, blah, but I don't buy it. My own childhood was terrible. My parents were jerks (today, society would call them abusive), and I didn't have much fun growing up. I always felt like a mini-adult, having to take too much responsibility for my younger siblings. I can hardly remember any good times; it was a terrible childhood. I wasn't joyfully optimistic."

"Listen carefully, Harry," corrected Tanaka, "I didn't say childhood is always wonderful. I said the spirit of a child is fun, authentic, true, natural, and full of joyful optimism. Unfortunately, parents and other grown-ups often mess it up for children. Many parents bring their own personal neurosis—their fears, resentments, addictions, and superstitions—into their role as parents. Instead of giving their children abundant love with reasonable limits, these misguided parents give their children their own negativity—their fears, doubts, and pains. An insidious pattern now emerges: Addictive parents raise addictive children. Cold and abusive parents raise cold and abusive children. The cycle continues for generations, with no end in sight.

"Fortunately, this self-destructive cycle can be reversed into a positive pattern—parents can also help create a positive influence of love, growth, and success in their children.

"For example, enlightened parents—those who are dedicated to improving themselves, psychologically and spiritually—don't let their personal traumas and painful pasts affect their children. Instead, they prepare a safe and beautiful emotional place for their children to grow and develop openness, truthfulness, security, love, and above all, Joyful Optimism.

"Remember, Harry, when I said that humans are asleep, thinking they're awake? That's very true. And, the sad part is that if you tell humans they're asleep or deluded they will deny it with all of their hearts, and they will even become angry with you for telling them."

"Why is that, teacher?" Harry was eager to learn more.

"Because only awakened human beings realize they have been dreaming; people don't know they're in a dream until they wake up. Many deluded humans dream themselves into believing they are actually quite happy and successful, when the reality is that they're deeply miserable inside. Although they may not yet realize it, they've lost the happiness, spark, and intuitive genius of the childhood spirit. It's gone for them."

Harry started to think deeply; he was starting to see the truth. "Yes, you're right; many of my patients lack that amazing childhood spirit, and I must admit, I lack it, too." Harry suddenly had a thought, a slim ray of hope. "But, I know that optimism is there, somewhere, deep inside of me. Please, tell me: Is there a way for me to recapture the joyful optimism of the childhood spirit? Is it possible for me, still?"

Tanaka was pensive, and spoke slowly—making sure Harry understood exactly what he needed to do. "Yes, you can recapture Joyful Optimism, Harry. It doesn't matter if you had a wonderfully joyous childhood, or a lousy, pain-filled one. Right now, at this very moment, you can implant the joy of the childhood spirit in your mind.

"Try this exercise: See yourself as a small child again. Imagine yourself with the same face, hands, feet, and body you had when you were little. Now, imagine that you're going to fill that child's heart (your heart) with joy unimaginable. Think of all the enthusiasm, love, playfulness, and spontaneity you have observed and experienced in the world, and imagine that this child, this YOU, has all of this wonder, passion, and spontaneity in his heart, right at this very moment. See yourself as this child—smiling, laughing, running, and playing—drinking from the intoxicating nectar of an unlimited and beautiful future. That is you, right now, Harry. The child in you—you in the child.

"Harry, believe me when I tell you this: The more you imagine this happy and joyous child within you, the more positive changes you will see in your own life. Your smile will grow wider, your laughter will be more sincere and intoxicating; your mind will be more clear, gentle, and innocent. And, one day, Harry, it will all come together for you. On that momentous occasion, you will rejoice because joyful optimism has entered your heart fully, and it will stay with you for the rest of your life."

Chapter Six

The Final Secret: Forgiveness

"Harry, we have learned the first two secrets: Gratitude, which energizes our present, and Joyful Optimism, which secures our future. But, now we must deal with perhaps the most important key for our ultimate happiness. It is called Forgiveness. The forgiveness that heals our past and prepares our future."

"How do you define forgiveness, teacher?" asked Harry.

"Forgiveness is the process of wiping your mental and spiritual slate clean of all the harms that have been done to you. If someone has injured you in the past, by forgiving that person, you no longer harbor any ill will or resentment toward him or her; you have erased the pain of what was done to you. You are now free to offer compassion to that person, not because he or she deserves it, but because you are a God-created human being who has mercy and compassion within you.

"Harry, think back to that incredible moment in history when the Lover of Humanity was being crucified, and he whispered those precious words to his captors—a bittersweet song that resonated forever throughout the echo of eternity: 'Father, forgive them, for they do not know what they are doing.'

"Imagine, Harry, if you can, the magnitude of what happened on that cross: This Man of Forever was forgiving those who had tortured and humiliated him; the very men who would kill him in the worst way possible. He was forgiving these murderers, the worst of the worst, offering love in place of hate; compassion in place of condemnation.

"And, Harry, I will tell you something else. When Jesus forgave those torturers and murderers, he was creating the perfect example for us. He was setting us free from the frozen pain of our past; from those who have hurt and betrayed us; from those who have tried to infect us with the diseases of hate, prejudice, superstition, and fear.

"Forgiveness. What a beautiful idea; but, unfortunately, one that's so difficult to carry out in real life. It's not so easy to forgive, is it, Harry? You know that as well as anyone. Tell me, can you forgive your abusive parents? The teacher who humiliated you? The 'best friend' who stabbed you in the back? The ex-wife who took everything you had and left you spent and bitter?"

"Teacher, I know exactly what you're talking about; forgiveness is so difficult for me." Harry was struggling for words. This was harder than he had imagined. "I still have hidden resentment and anger toward those who hurt me in the past. The pain is still there, very much alive inside me. Why can't I forgive?"

"Harry, I'm going to tell you a hard truth right now. You may not like this, but here it is: You don't forgive because you secretly love your resentment—yes, you do.

"Deep inside; you love feeling like a 'poor me' victim. You love being the aggrieved person, the injured party. You don't admit this, of course. You pretend that you are all over that; you have grown up; you have matured. But, deep down, you are still just like a little child who feels you've been wronged. You keep insisting that other people pay for the sins they have committed against you.

"Don't get me wrong, Harry: I realize that, in certain circumstances in the past, you have been an innocent victim. Others have deceived, betrayed, and abused you without justification. Evil, cruel, and heartless people have hurt you, Harry, and to be honest with you, they probably don't deserve much, if any, mercy, kindness, or forgiveness.

"But, despite what they did to you—regardless of how much you suffered at their hands—you must still forgive them, Harry. You need to forgive those who harmed you, not because they deserve forgiveness, but because you deserve to experience the true joy and incredible freedom of forgiving others. It's true, the more you forgive, the more you are healed.

"Also, remember that forgiveness is blind to the type of wrong or injury committed. Forgiveness forgives all, even the worst of the worst. The most inhumane and horrible treatment ever endured can be forgiven. If Jesus did it, you can too because you were created from the same mold: Love.

"You see, Harry, forgiveness is the greatest love of all—it is love's highest form. Forgiveness takes self-interest, self-concern, and self-pity completely out of the picture. It completely eliminates the false, temporarily reassuring feeling we get when we play the victim role— the erroneous belief that the world owes us something because of the bad way we've been treated.

"No, Harry, the world doesn't owe us anything. We owe the world our forgiveness. And, the more we pay the debt, the more emotionally wealthy we will be. We will no longer be bound by the anger, resentments, and hostilities of the past. We will liberate ourselves from the cruel, from the malicious, from the evil. The ones who hurt us in the past can't harm us anymore because we have taken away the only things they could hold us with: anger, resentment, and hate. Does this make sense?"

"Yes, I guess," Harry said weakly.

"Stop fighting yourself, Harry. Forgive those who have harmed you, in any way, shape, or form. Do it right now. Forgive. That teacher. That parent. That friend. That lover. That public role model. Forgive anyone you think has let you down, hurt you, or betrayed you.

"Don't do it for them. Do it for yourself so you can see clearly through the eyes of love, instead of through the clouded lens of anger, resentment, and hate. Do this, and you will feel better, much better, I promise you. Do this, and you will experience love in its purest form: Unconditional love, Agape.

"Harry, know this: When you forgive others, you are not condoning what they did to you. You're not accepting their lifestyle, their behavior, or their choices. You don't even have to like them; you don't have to associate with them in any way. But, you do need to forgive them because that is the only true love you have left."

"This is powerful stuff," said Harry, as he finally understood what forgiveness was all about. It made absolute, perfect sense.

"Yes, it is powerful, Harry, but I have saved the best for last. I must now tell you about a very large obstacle to your success and happiness in life; a stumbling block so great that we must address it now. Otherwise, I'm afraid the three keys may be useless to you."

"Please tell me what it is." Harry was truly concerned now; this must be important.

"Harry," began Tanaka somberly, "This stumbling block I'm talking about is the mental place where you have buried all of your failures, mistakes, and poor choices. You buried them, Harry, but they are still there, like zombies, ready to come alive at night, when you're just about to fall asleep. You start dozing off for a second, and here come those sneaky suckers—those hideous mental zombies. Their game: To torment you into an early mental death. Their name: Regret.

"Regret, Harry. It's the worst feeling of all—that nagging, self-attacking torment that reminds you of your most horrendous mistakes, that brings to mind your terrible failures. Your unrealized dreams, Harry, your failed possibilities. Regret scolds you when it tells you that you blew your opportunities and ruined your life. Regret taunts you when it says you can never get back what you lost; you will never have what you really want.

"The funny thing is that you may not have actually done anything wrong. Maybe you didn't make any real mistakes or errors. But, Regret isn't having any of that. Regret makes you feel like you've made terrible, and irreparable mistakes, even if you really didn't. Always quick with damning questions—Why did you?; Why didn't you?—Regret makes you second-guess everything in your life:

"Why did you stay with that stupid, abusive, and incompatible partner who made your existence a living hell?

"Why didn't you stay with that awesome soul mate—the one true love of your life?

"Why did you continue working at that miserable job you hated—that career you loathed?

"Why didn't you follow your dream and become a(n) (scientist. . .entrepreneur. . .lawyer. . .doctor. . .homemaker. . .artist. . .musician. . .craftsperson. . .teacher. . .fill in the blank)?

"Why? Regret screams.

"But, you don't have a good answer, do you Harry? The only good answer, Regret tells you, is that you are a stupid, foolish, and worthless piece of excrement.

"Never letting you rest, never letting you feel satisfied and contented, Regret liberally sprinkles the word 'should' in all of its conversations with you—making you suffer all the more. It taunts you, 'You should have saved more money (or enjoyed your money more)'; 'You should have invested more (or invested less)'; 'You should have lived there (or not lived there)'; 'You should have worked there (or not worked there)'; 'You should have said that (or not said that)'; 'You should have loved that person (or not loved that person)'; and the list goes on and on.

"Regrets, you've had more than a few. Isn't that true, Harry?"

"Yes, teacher, it's very true," said Harry with a heavy heart, as he staggered under the twin tonnage of bitterness and regret. "One of my biggest regrets, in fact, was losing the love of my life, Daphne, to my own stupidity. Beautiful Daphne. I can still taste the sweet scent of her skin; feel her touch upon me, hear her gentle voice. But, I blew it with her. We were both so young, and I was too immature—too rude, rough, and jealous with her. I knew I made a big mistake; I should have let our love grow gently and patiently; we could still be together now, we would be so much in love. I wish..."

"Stop it!" screamed Tanaka as he unleashed a backhand strike to Harry's face.

Stunned, more than hurt by the blow, Harry began to cry.

"I'm such a loser," said Harry, with extreme self-pity and heartache suffocating his every breath. "I didn't deserve her. I don't deserve anything. I've made so many mistakes in my life—I've hurt so many people."

Again, Tanaka raised his hand as if to strike Harry. Only this time, he laid it, ever so gently, on Harry's cheek, as he whispered two simple, pure, beautiful words in his ear: "Forgive yourself."

Before Tanaka touched his cheek, Harry had been lost in his self-indulgent reverie of regret. In his mind's eye, he clearly saw all of the people he had hurt in his life. He painfully unearthed all of those hidden thoughts of failure and shame and guilt and regret—cringing as they washed over him like a great, unrelenting ocean wave. Harry was so wrapped up in his own mind, in fact, that he barely heard when Tanaka whispered the beautiful, merciful, and melodic words in his ear—so faintly, so softly, so gently, "Forgive yourself." But, now the words—"Forgive Yourself" finally began sinking into Harry's consciousness. He suddenly stopped crying and looked at Tanaka with a mixture of hope and expectation.

Tanaka knew exactly the pain Harry was feeling. He offered words of support and healing directly from his heart, "My son, my friend, my love: Forgiveness of others is hard for some, but true forgiveness of self is nearly impossible for many. We are often our own worst enemies; our most severe critics. While we can sometimes find it in our hearts to forgive others, we don't often extend that same tenderness, love, and courtesy to ourselves for our real or imagined mistakes. We are too critical, too rough, too harsh on ourselves.

"This self-criticism becomes ingrained in our mind from an early age. It takes the form of our parents' voices who tell us, 'You're a sinner; you're going to hell.' 'You're too irresponsible; you'll never make it on your own.' 'You're not loving; you won't find anyone to love you.'

"On and on, the voices torment us, as we incorporate them into our minds as real entities, otherwise known as Thought Demons—the evil, self-defeating voices from within.

"The Regret Thought Demon is an especially tough foe when it comes to Self-Forgiveness. It is so hard to be kind to ourselves. We're often kinder to strangers than we are to ourselves because we don't see that our true nature is really made of love and forgiveness, not regret.

"Now, Harry, I want you to do something at this very moment that will help you wipe out regret from your life. Are you ready?"

"Yes, teacher," said Harry, eager to rid himself of that terrible enemy—Regret—once and for all.

"I want you to go back in time mentally to that point of regret when you lost your first love, Daphne. See yourself as you were then— alone with your pain, regretting what you had done in the relationship, tormenting yourself with the thoughts, 'How could I have been such a fool? I will never love like that again.'

"Harry, do you see yourself the way you were then?"

"Yes," said Harry as his eyes filled with bitterness and tears.

"OK, now I want you to see the 'You' of today (in your present bodily form) sitting face to face with the younger you.

"Do you see that?"

"Yes."

"OK, good," continued Tanaka. "Next, I want you to visualize the older 'You' saying to the younger 'You' these three simple words: 'I forgive you.' Visualize, now, that the two Yous (your younger self and your present self) are hugging each other to the rhythm of for-giveness—rocking, flowing, and harmonizing."

After a few minutes of meditation and contemplation, Harry opened his eyes. Tanaka asked him if he had been able to do the exercise, and what he had felt. Harry was clear-eyed, and he felt warmly relaxed. He answered, "Yes, I saw it; I experienced it. It was an amazing thing, both of us—my past and my present selves—coming together like that, forgiving each other, supporting each other, caring for each other. I can't explain exactly how I feel right now; I just feel different, lighter, more at peace."

"What else?" asked Tanaka. Tanaka knew Harry had changed. Now he wanted to know exactly how much.

"The regret is no longer there, teacher," said Harry in a calm and steady voice. "It's completely gone; I can't quite believe it. At first, I couldn't shake the regret of losing Daphne. But then, during the exercise, I thought about her in a completely different way, and this time, I realized the end of our relationship happened for a purpose; we were not meant to be together. She now has a wonderful married life with the soul mate she truly loves and deserves. I'm happy for her, I really am. I have no regrets."

Now finished with what he had to say, his heart finally released, Harry allowed his head to fall on Tanaka's shoulder, as Tanaka's large arms wrapped themselves around Harry, and both started to cry tears of forgiveness, love, and happiness. At that very moment, something miraculous happened. The end became the beginning, the past joined the future, and most wonderful of all, Regret merged into Forgiveness—giving Harry the greatest gift of all: Love.

Chapter Seven

Postscript: A World of Happiness

One week after their momentous meeting, Tanaka passed to a different plane of existence—transforming in his sleep from life to death. Few attended Tanaka's funeral; not many knew him, although many had heard about him. Harry came to pay his respects, but he didn't stay very long. Tanaka would not have wanted any regrets, Harry was sure of that.

As for Harry, he never did write that chapter in his autobiography about the "Happiness Man in the Wilderness." In fact, Harry never did write his autobiography at all. He decided he still had too much living to do—not the kind of living he had done before, but true, happy living. Along the way, Harry scaled down his therapy practice, bought himself a small cabin in the mountains, and began spending many fun and relaxed days and nights in his wilderness vacation home.

Now, on starry night after starry night, Harry lay on the ground near his cabin, listening to the harmonious and lovely sounds of nature. And, it was on one of those particularly beautiful nights that Harry looked up into the sky and recognized something strangely familiar; something comfortably sweet. It was up there, yes, he was sure of that; a vision of something special—a form without form; visible, yet invisible, this thing (it had no name) floating among the trees, the birds, the rocks, and the sky. Then, he recognized something else; this form without form was laughing with unrestrained joy, and pointing three long, tender fingers toward him. Each finger, one feeling. Each finger, one Secret: Gratitude, Optimism, and yes, Forgiveness. How could Harry ever forget? The Author had written it for him—right there, in his soul, right there, in his heart.

About

DR. ALEXANDER AVILA

Dr. Alexander Avila holds four graduate degrees, including a Ph.D. in clinical psychology. He is the bestselling author of *Love-Types* (Avon Books) and *The Gift of Shyness* (Simon and Schuster). *LoveTypes* is the first book to teach readers how to find their compatible soul mate from among the 16 Myers-Briggs personality types. Over 40 million Internet users have applied Dr. Avila's Love-Type system to find lasting love. *The Gift of Shyness* has broken new ground by showing shy and Introverted singles how to embrace their Introversion and Shyness to develop social confidence and attract their ideal love partner.

As a respected college professor, researcher, and presenter, Dr. Avila has shared his findings with students, academics, and professionals in the fields of psychology and human behavioral sciences.

An acclaimed TV and Radio Personality, Dr. Avila is the creator of the award-winning show, Love University, in which listeners learn how to love themselves, others, and a higher power. He has appeared on numerous media outlets such as *CNN, ABC, CBS, and Telemundo*, and has been featured in *Cosmopolitan, Glamour, Latina, Today's Black Woman, Real Health, Woman's World*, and the *Los Angeles Times*, among other publications.

On a personal note, Dr. Avila enjoys salsa dancing, chess, books, good-hearted people, martial arts, animals, nature, and spirituality.

Dr. Avila's mission is to help humanity transform pain into power and to extend loving energy to the world. Dr. Avila can be reached at **3secretsofhappiness@gmail.com**

Join Dr. Avila each week for a fun and practical weekly lesson on self-empowerment and love on his hit podcast, Love University.

In school, you learned about grammar, history, science, and math, but chances are you weren't educated on some of the most important things in life: love, relationships, success, and happiness.

In Love University, Dr. Avila teaches you how to achieve mastery in your relationships, finances, career, health, and emotional well-being. Utilizing a unique blend of positive psychology, practical spirituality, and plain old common sense, Love University shows you how to love yourself, others, and a higher nature.

Some of the popular topics include:

- *The Psychology of Wealth: How to Have the Mind of Abundance*
- *Find Your Mate With the Power of Personality Type*
- *Co-Dependency for Dummies: Set Yourself Free*
- *Humor IQ: Laugh Your Way to Joy and Success*
- *The Power of Self-Discipline: The Might to Do Right*
- *The Abuse-Free Life: Declare Your Emotional Freedom*
- *Personal Spirituality: Your Path to Joy and Inner Power*
- *Be the Ruler of Technology, Not Its Servant*

Listen each Wednesday as Dr. Avila, the Professor of the Heart, and his celebrity guests, entertain, educate, and enlighten you on the secrets of love, success, and happiness.

Love University is now in session.

LISTEN ON ITUNES: https://apple.co/2FjNOYo
LISTEN ON PODBEAN: loveuniversity.podbean.com

JOIN THE "TYPE COMMUNITY" AND FIND THE LOVE OF YOR LIFE

Now there's a way to win the love game and find the right man for you: It's called *GuyTypes*.

In *GuyTypes*, bestselling author and award-winning psychologist, Dr. Alexander Avila, introduces a revolutionary new love finding paradigm. Streamlining his classic bestseller *LoveTypes* (over 40 million followers), and combining social networking with Myers-Briggs Type compatibility, Dr. Avila unveils a groundbreaking system for finding true love in our fast-paced technological world. In *GuyTypes*, you will discover what you truly want in a guy and how to get it. Here are the four GuyTypes (romantic styles) who can light your fire and keep it burning. One of these will be your perfect match (you will learn which one):

Meaning Seeker (NF): 13.5% of the male population. If you've ever wanted to be romanced like a goddess, then this is the right guy for you. Sensitive, imaginative, artistic, philosophical, poetic, and a true romantic: He is the lover of all lovers.

Knowledge Seeker (NT): 14.8% of the male population. You've met your "Iron Man": Brilliant, powerful, innovative, and ultimately successful. His incredible brainpower will stimulate your mind (and body), and his incisive and witty take on life will keep you intrigued and fascinated.

Security Seeker (SJ): 43.1% of the male population. You've found your rock: steady, reliable, traditional, and family-orientated. He is the loyal husband and loving father who will be by your side for life; there is nothing he won't do for you and the family he loves.

Excitement Seeker (SP): 28.6% of the male population. Get ready and fasten your seatbelts—the fun is about to begin. This charismatic and confident guy will bring as much fun, laughter, and enjoyment into your life together as humanly possible.

Once you know the right guy for you, you will learn how to:

*Quickly profile his personality type by asking 3 Magic questions or making micro-observations about his behavior.

*Use Personality Networking and the latest social media tools to break the ice and get to know him.

*Win his heart by tapping into his unique personality type preferences.

*Rate his sexual compatibility (including cheating risk), fatherhood ability, and long-term relationship potential.

*Develop a lasting relationship and marriage with the love of your life.

Go here to obtain your copy of *GuyTypes* and finally find the man you can love for a lifetime: **http://www.guytypes.com/my-books/**

READ THE BOOK THAT STARTED THE DATING REVOLUTION AND FIND YOUR SOUL MATE TODAY: *LOVETYPES: DISCOVER YOUR ROMANTIC STYLE AND FIND YOUR SOUL MATE*

Now there's a solution to incompatible dates and failed relationships: It's called *LoveTypes: Discover Your Romantic Style and Find Your Soul Mate* by Dr. Alexander Avila.

With over 40 million followers, and 20 years of proven love compatibility results, *LoveTypes* is your go-to guide to help you find your soul mate from among the crowd of potential suitors. Dr. Avila has revolutionized the dating world by applying the theory behind the Myers-Briggs Type Indicator®—the most popular personality test in the world—to teach readers how to find their most compatible partner from among the 16 LoveTypes, or romantic styles.

By taking a brief quiz, you first determine your unique LoveType profile. From there, the system guides you toward the best Love-Type for you and provides specific answers to your most pressing relationship questions:

*Which of the 16 *LoveTypes* is most compatible with me—psychologically, emotionally, and sexually?

*What four questions can I ask to determine instantly if someone is right for me?

*Where can I meet my ideal mate?

*What dating strategies will win the heart of my ideal LoveType and ensure a long-term relationship?

Lasting love no longer has to be hit or miss with *LoveTypes*, your complete and indispensable guide to a happy and fulfilling romantic life.

TO FIND YOUR SOUL MATE TODAY, GO HERE FOR YOUR COPY OF *LOVETYPES*:
http://www.guytypes.com/my-books/

Made in the USA
Columbia, SC
04 November 2022

70422279R00028